Erin Silver

MIGHTY SCARED

The AMAZING Ways Animals DEFEND Themselves

illustrated by
Hayden Maynard

ORCA BOOK PUBLISHERS

Are you afraid of the dark? Of getting lost? Of something you saw in a movie? Maybe someone laughed at you for being scared or called you a chicken. That's okay! Being scared is natural and helpful. In fact, it's how we stay safe. While people might run or scream, animals have cool ways of protecting themselves when they're afraid—ways that are amazing… and amazingly awesome. So what do animals do when they get mighty scared?

PISTOL SHRIMP
Shoot bubble bullets

Location: *Worldwide*
Habitat: *Coral and oyster reefs, seagrass flats and* **estuaries**
Special feature: *One claw is bigger than the other and up to half the length of its body.*

WHEN THEY GET SCARED:
When a pistol shrimp gets scared, it snaps its large claw shut at 100 miles (160 kilometers) per hour. It's so fast that the snapping motion creates a pocket of air, or bubble bullet, that shoots through the water. When the bubble explodes, the force of it stuns or kills enemies on contact. That burst of water is as hot as the sun and louder than fireworks.

GET TO KNOW ME

What scares you?
I'm as big as a fish stick. That's right—I'm only 1 to 2 inches (2.5 to 5 centimeters) long. I can be eaten by bigger, hungry sea creatures, like hawkfish, groupers and lionfish.

How do you fight back?
I'm a sharp-shooting underwater cowboy with the fastest claw in the sea. I'm great at catching small shrimp, crabs, fish and snails, also known as dinner. But when an enemy comes near, I'll fire a bubble bullet their way—they won't even know what hit 'em. Yeehaw!

Any other cool facts you want to share?
When my friends and I shoot bubble bullets, we can disrupt **sonar** and underwater communication. Humans don't like the noise and blame us for letting enemy submarines sneak into their territory. I might be a cowboy, but I'm no match for the military!

HAGFISH
Slime their attackers

Habitat: Cold waters around the world
Diet: Spineless sea creatures and dead marine life
Appearance: Its long, slender body is made entirely of cartilage.

WHEN THEY GET SCARED:
When a hagfish is scared by predators, its body makes snot—less than a teaspoon (5 milliliters) at first. But before you can snap your fingers, the goo grows 10,000 times larger—that's enough to fill a bucket. These strands of slime are thinner than human hair, stronger than nylon stockings and very flexible. When mixed with seawater the slime expands so much it can smother attackers.

GET TO KNOW ME

What scares you?
I go mushy just thinking about my enemies—eels, fish and sharks. And can you believe it? In Korea we are stir-fried and eaten in a dish called kkomjangeo bokkeum. I'm curling up now...

How do you fight back?
When I get scared, pores on my body make slime. Tons of it. It's so strong, it can clog a *predator*'s gills and even suffocate a shark. That's when I say, "Buh-bye!" Scientists think they can use my slime to make clothes. Have their people call my people.

Any other cool facts you want to share?
Well, it's sort of embarrassing, but if you come a little closer, I'll whisper it: Sometimes I accidentally slime myself. I have to tie myself into a knot to work the goop down and off my body. Whoopsie!

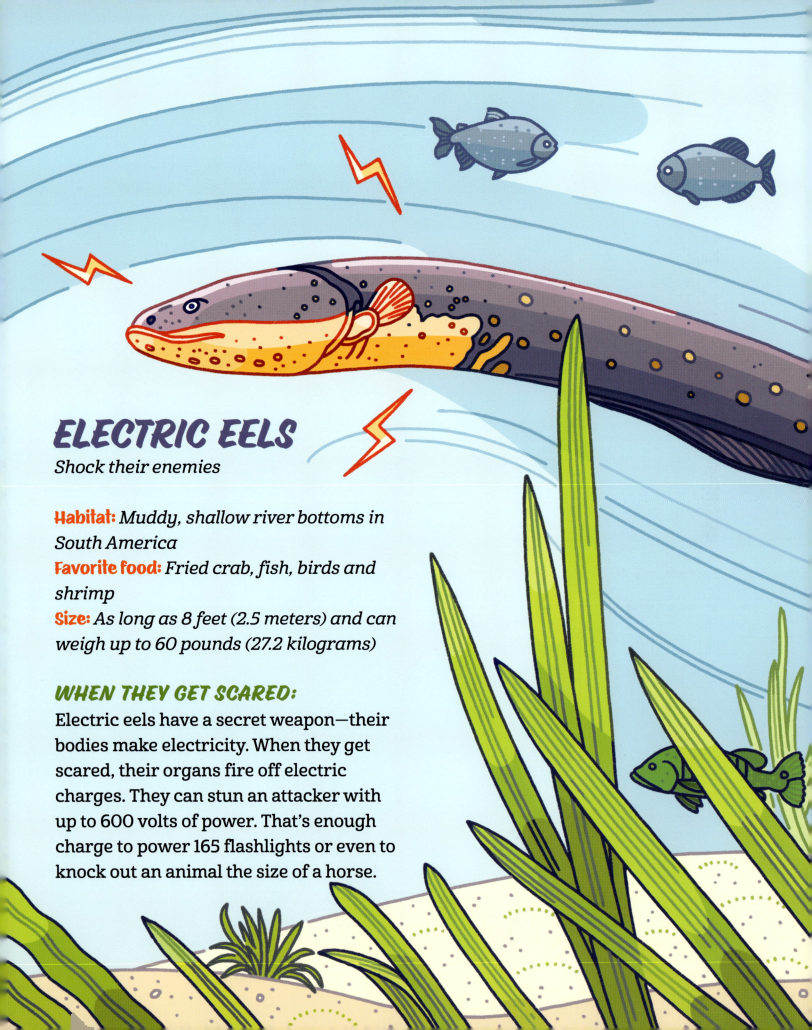

ELECTRIC EELS
Shock their enemies

Habitat: *Muddy, shallow river bottoms in South America*

Favorite food: *Fried crab, fish, birds and shrimp*

Size: *As long as 8 feet (2.5 meters) and can weigh up to 60 pounds (27.2 kilograms)*

WHEN THEY GET SCARED:
Electric eels have a secret weapon—their bodies make electricity. When they get scared, their organs fire off electric charges. They can stun an attacker with up to 600 volts of power. That's enough charge to power 165 flashlights or even to knock out an animal the size of a horse.

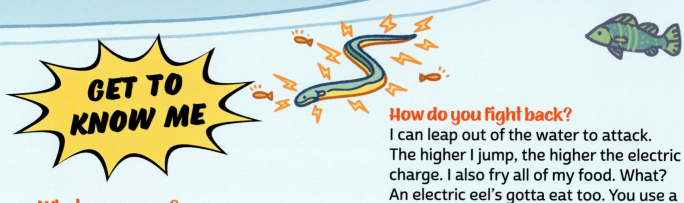

GET TO KNOW ME

What scares you?
Please don't ask me that! It's too scary. Okay, fine. I'll tell you. I'm scared of crocodiles, jaguars and leopards. When the water gets shallow, or when I come up for air, I feel afraid. I might live in water and have gills, but I need to breathe once every 10 minutes. It's so stressful.

How do you fight back?
I can leap out of the water to attack. The higher I jump, the higher the electric charge. I also fry all of my food. What? An electric eel's gotta eat too. You use a microwave, don't you?

Any other cool facts you want to share?
If you think I'm electrifying, you should meet my cousins. I'm related to 21 **species** of electric catfish from Africa. If you're ever in the Nile River, you should say hi. Or, on second thought, maybe you shouldn't...

BOX JELLYFISH
Stun predators

Life span: *3 to 12 months*
Maximum swim speed: *Up to 5 miles (8 kilometers) per hour*
Diet: *Small fish, worms and even other jellyfish*

WHEN THEY GET SCARED:
A box jellyfish can grow as many as 15 **tentacles** from the corners of its head. Each tentacle can be up to 10 feet (3 meters) long, and have 5,000 stinging cells filled with **venom** that can stun and even kill enemies. That's why some species of box jellyfish are called the deadliest jellyfish in the world.

GET TO KNOW ME

What scares you?
Any sea creature that tries to attack me will get what's coming to them. Look out, butterfish, batfish and crabs. But yikes—there's a sea turtle. My sting doesn't affect them. Oh no...I've got to go.

How do you fight back?
I'm bluish and see-through, which makes me hard to spot. But if I feel threatened, I'll reach out with my tentacles and *zzzzzaaaaappppp*! When I'm hunting for a meal, I use my stinging cells to paralyze my food. Then I use my tentacles like hands to shovel food into my mouth. Hey—don't look at me like that. I'm still a jellyfish, not a pig!

Any other cool facts you want to share?
I'm related to a jellyfish that sends shivers down *my* spine—well, it would if I had a spine. The biggest, deadliest jellyfish is called *Chironex fleckeri.* He's killed at least 64 people since 1883.

PYGMY SPERM WHALES
Squirt ink

Habitat: *Warm waters*
Status: *It's rare to see one, so researchers don't know much about them.*
Appearance: *Dark backs and light bellies help* **camouflage** *them.*

WHEN THEY GET SCARED:
When they get scared, pygmy sperm whales squirt ink from their butt (also called the *lower intestinal tract*). They can produce about 3 gallons (11 liters) of ink, that's more than a jug of milk. The reddish-brown liquid makes it hard for their enemies to see in the water. That's when these whales make their escape.

GET TO KNOW ME

What scares you?
Do you really have to ask? Look at the size of me! Compared to great white sharks and killer whales, I look like a goldfish.

How do you fight back?
Sometimes I'll be minding my own business, looking for squid, octopuses, crabs, shrimp or fish, using **echolocation,** when all of a sudden a shadow appears. I get so scared that I—*pfffttttt*! My intestines squirt a cloud of ink to "muddy the water," so to speak. That's why my friends and I never watch *Shark Week* during sleepovers.

Any other cool facts you want to share?
When I release my ink, some people think I'm pooping in the water, but that fluid is inky, just like the squid's. Yes, it comes from my behind, but still...I'm not a poopy-pants!

ASSASSIN BUGS
Wear dead bodies

Location: *All over the world*
How they got their name: *They'll do anything to catch and kill a meal.*
Who loves them: *Gardeners. They eat pests that feed on garden flowers.*

WHEN THEY GET SCARED:

An assassin bug uses its nose like a straw. It stabs its prey and sucks out its insides. Then it wears the victim's hard shell on its back. The shell works like a protective shield to hide the assassin bug's smell from its enemies and as a disguise to catch unsuspecting bugs. Some kinds of assassin bugs have two types of venom: one to defend themselves against predators and the second to paralyze and liquefy their prey.

GET TO KNOW ME

What scares you?
They call me Assassin. Assassin Bug. And yes, I'm short—I won't grow much bigger than 1 inch (2.5 centimeters). That means countless enemies are out to get me…spiders, rodents, birds. Even other assassin bugs. I have to be on high alert.

How do you fight back?
I've been trained to go on the attack when I'm scared. Take a look at my dead-bug backpack. No, I'm not going to school. The backpack helps me complete my missions undetected. And do you see my legs? I can dip them in tree sap to attract and kill bees. You don't want to get tangled up in these hairy, sticky things. If you do, it's game over.

Any other cool facts you want to share?
There are 6,600 species of assassin bugs. If we had a big family dinner, we'd eat ants, termites and bees. But, of course, the location of our next gathering is top secret.

TEXAS HORNED LIZARDS
Shoot blood

Location: *Texas, but now mostly extinct*
Habitat: *Hot, dry, sandy places*
Diet: *Red ants*

WHEN THEY GET SCARED:
Texas horned lizards have two horns and spiky scales. When they're afraid, these lizards puff up so they look too big to swallow. At night they hide in the sand to stay safe. But this lizard has one other trick. By raising its blood pressure, it can make blood vessels in its eyelids burst and shoot a stream of blood at its enemies. Predators get confused and the blood tastes disgusting.

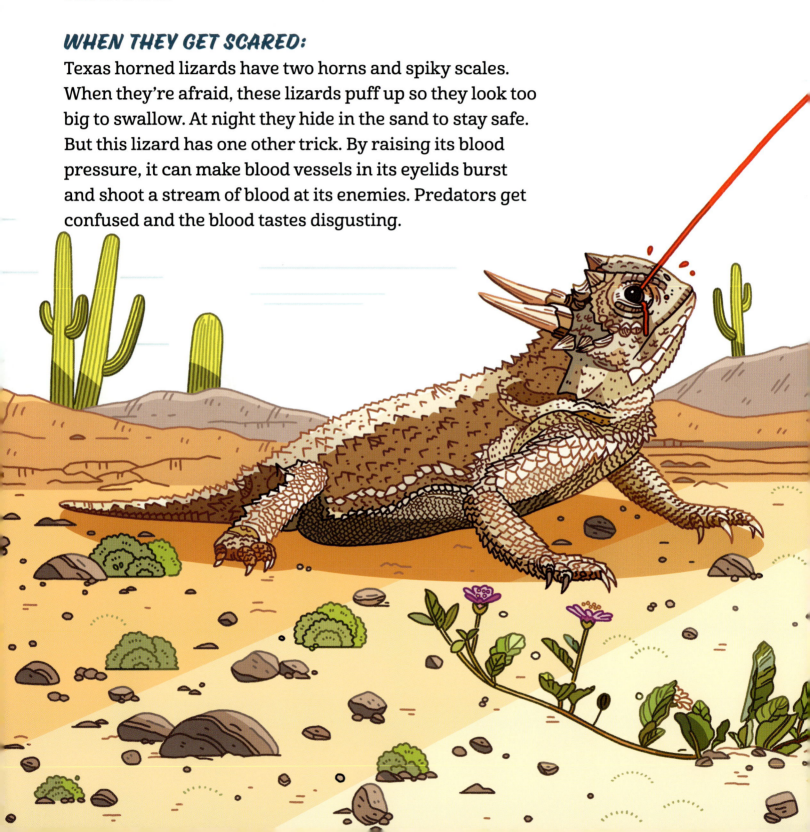

GET TO KNOW ME

What scares you?
Looking in the mirror. I'm hideous! But I also get scared when I'm hunted by snakes, wolves and coyotes. If I don't act fast, I'll be Texas toast!

How do you fight back?
I hide or make myself look extra big and scary—not easy for a lizard that's flat and shorter than the length of a finger. But I can do one other thing few lizards can do—I shoot blood from my eyes. Don't mess with Texas!

Any other cool facts you want to share?
Okay, there's one other thing I didn't mention. My defenses are powerless against people. I'm now a threatened species in Texas thanks to **pesticides** that have poisoned my family and made red ants disappear. They were my favorite food. That means there aren't many of us left, and I need **conservationists** to save me.

OPOSSUMS
Pretend they're dead

Birth: *Litters of up to 20 joeys*
Size: *Born the size of a bee but grow as big as a small dog*
Teeth: *They have 50 teeth, more than any other* **mammal** *in North America.*

WHEN THEY GET SCARED:
An opossum bares its teeth and hisses at attackers to look scary. But it also rolls over and plays dead. It stares off into space, drools from its mouth and blows bubbles out its nose. Opossums even release a disgusting stink from their behinds. They look (and smell) so unappetizing that predators leave them alone.

GET TO KNOW ME

What scares you?
I'm such a good actor, I should win an Oscar. If only there were a category for Best Performing Animal. When I'm off searching for food in dumpsters, backyards and garbage cans, I get scared by animals like dogs, cats and foxes. They're always after me!

How do you fight back?
After my "death-defying" performance, I pop back to life. Sometimes it takes me a few hours to unfreeze before I take my bow. But I'm not just a skilled actor. I also have **opposable thumbs**. My sharp claws and long tail help me climb trees and dig homes.

Any other cool facts you want to share?
For my encore, you should know that my body temperature is so low that viruses like rabies can't survive in me. Since I don't get sick, the show can go on! Venomous scorpion and snake bites don't affect me either, and scientists want to know why.

CAMELS
Kick and spit

Location: *North Africa and the Middle East*
Diet: *Grass, grains and even prickly cactus plants*
Strength: *They can carry up to 600 pounds (272 kilograms) on their backs.*

WHEN THEY GET SCARED:
When this "ship of the desert" gets scared, its cheeks bulge with saliva and food from its stomach. Then a camel spits at its enemies to surprise and distract them. Its kick is strong enough to kill a predator. You don't want to get bitten either—a camel's teeth and jaws are as strong as a wolf's.

GET TO KNOW ME

What scares you?
I'll be honest—I used to be scared of predators in the wild, like lions, tigers and wolves. Today people need us for milk, wool and transportation, so we're mostly kept safe. My two-humped cousins, Bactrian camels in China and Mongolia, however, are *endangered*. They're hunted by people for fun and food. It makes me so mad I could spit.

How do you fight back?
If I need to get away, I can run 40 miles (64 kilometers) per hour. In a 100-meter race, even the fastest human would be left in my dust. Ha!

Any other cool facts you want to share?
I can last about two weeks without water and a few months without a meal. When I'm thirsty, I can drink 32 gallons (145 liters) of water in 13 minutes. That's like filling up two large cars at the gas station!

HORSEFLIES
Speed away

Favorite season: *Most active in summer*
Babies: Larvae *tear and eat insects, worms, snails and other larvae.*
Diet: *Flower nectar and blood from horses, cows, deer and people*

WHEN THEY GET SCARED:
Horseflies live around the world and are like giant, bloodthirsty mosquitos. The females have mouths that stab and saw through flesh and suck up blood, which they need to lay eggs. When they are scared by a predator or even a shadow, they zoom away.

GET TO KNOW ME

What scares you?
I work so hard to be a good mother. I drink as much blood as I can to lay 1,000 healthy eggs at once. But I get scared when my little larvae are eaten by animals like birds, flies and worms. Even I could be devoured by birds and wasps.

How do you fight back?
By making a speedy getaway, of course! Males can zoom off at 90 miles (145 kilometers) per hour. Some people are allergic to my saliva and can end up with health problems. Sorry...sort of!

Any other cool facts you want to share?
My eyes can be tricked by stripes and patterns. I don't often bite horses with patterned blankets on their backs, and a zebra's stripes can confuse me.

JAPANESE HONEYBEES
Cook enemies

Habitat: *Japan's mountain areas*
Claim to fame: *Produce a rare honey that has a mild taste*
Defensive weapons: *Ambushing and bee balling*

WHEN THEY GET SCARED:
Japanese honeybees work together to fight enemies, like hornets, by forming a tight ball around the insect. It's a survival strategy called *bee balling*. It gets so hot inside the ball that enemies are roasted alive at 117°F (47°C) in under an hour. Their bodies can stand more heat than a hornet's, which means the Japanese honeybees don't overheat.

GET TO KNOW ME

What scares you?
I'm scared of the northern giant hornet. It's bigger than I am. If one gets inside our hive, it will mark the hive with its scent as a signal to its pals. Before we know it, a pack of up to 50 hornets will attack us inside our nest. Their powerful jawbones will cut off our heads and wipe us all out within hours. One bee can be killed every 14 seconds!

How do you fight back?
When we know attackers are coming, we wait at our hive until the hornets follow us inside. Then we bee ball 'em! Hundreds of us swarm the invader and cook 'em till they croak.

Any other cool facts you want to share?
We fertilize fruits, nuts, cauliflower, okra and onion. I bet you didn't know bees like cauliflower!

FULMAR BIRDS
Stink and vomit

Habitat: *North Atlantic, North Pacific and Southern Oceans*
Speed: *Up to 30 miles (47 kilometers) per hour*
Diet: *Fish, squid, shrimp, plankton and even garbage*

WHEN THEY GET SCARED:
Fulmar birds have a disgusting trick—they shoot an oily orange vomit at enemies. This barf can glue an enemy's feathers together, causing them to fall off a cliff and plunge into the water. The oil smells like garbage.

GET TO KNOW ME

What scares you?
When my parents leave me on our clifftop nest to find food, I can be easily attacked by birds, rats, squirrels or foxes. Mama!

How do you fight back?
Baby fulmars look helpless. But don't let our cuteness catch you off guard. I vomit at enemies to defend myself. That's actually how I got my name. *Fulmar* comes from two Old Norse words—*fúll* ("foul") and *már* ("gull"). I'm so stinky that a fulmar egg can still smell like rotten garbage 100 years after it's laid. Ha ha ha!

Any other cool facts you want to share?
My parents can eat their own vomit when they're out looking for food—it's like an energy bar.

FLYING SQUIRRELS
Glide through the air

Special feature: Nocturnal with night vision to spot food and enemies
Diet: Berries, nuts, fungi, seeds, insects, bird eggs and maple sap
Longest jump: 150 feet (46 meters) in one leap

WHEN THEY GET SCARED:
Flying squirrels call out to warn friends and scare enemies. They also camouflage themselves and stay still to blend in with trees and shadows. They stand tall and stretch to make themselves look bigger. Very speedy, they leap from tree to tree to escape predators. A special membrane between their front and back legs lets them glide—their legs steer and their tails are the brakes.

GET TO KNOW ME

What scares you?
Oh boy—great question. You might as well sit down and get comfy. I'm scared of coyotes, raccoons, weasels, cats, dogs, tree snakes, eagles, hawks, falcons and owls. I could go on, but I've got a flight to catch.

How do you fight back?
I love feeling free as a bird, but I don't actually have wings like one. Instead, when I get scared, I spread my arms and legs out wide and glide through the air like a kite. My jump can be as long as two bowling lanes. Sometimes it's hard to see me, but it's even harder to catch me!

Any other cool facts you want to share?
Skydivers have copied my moves. They jump out of planes wearing a flying-squirrel suit so they can glide just like me. This book is about scaredy-cats—it should be about copycats!

YOU

You can't zap an enemy when you're scared. You're not an electric eel! But you do have cool moves too. You can freeze to hide from danger, sort of like an opossum. Or you can make a loud noise, like a pistol shrimp. Being scared even helps you feel stronger and move faster, like a flying squirrel. Sometimes you might even feel like you have to go pee or poop. That's no accident. By getting rid of extra waste, your body can use its energy to escape from danger. Does this remind you of a pygmy sperm whale?

It's a good thing your body has an "off" switch. When you aren't in danger—like when the scary part of a movie is over—your body goes back to normal. To calm down, take deep breaths. This will slow your heart rate. Talk to someone you trust. Maybe you'll find there's nothing to be scared of after all. A relaxing activity, like going for a walk or thinking of a happy place, can also help. Ahhhh...that feels better!

GLOSSARY

camouflage—to disguise yourself to make it harder for others to see you

conservationists—people who help protect the environment and wildlife

echolocation—a process of locating objects using sound waves echoed back to the emitter, used by animals such as dolphins and bats

endangered—at risk of becoming extinct or disappearing

estuaries—an arm or inlet of the sea at the lower end of a river

larvae—plural of *larva*, an insect that's left its egg but hasn't yet developed into its adult form

mammal—animals (including people) that have hair or fur, are born live and are fed breast milk by their mothers

opposable thumbs—thumbs that can be moved around to touch the other fingers, making it possible for people (or animals) to grab objects with their hands

pesticides—chemicals or poisons used to kill bugs or stop them from eating plants and crops

predator—an animal that gets its food by killing other bugs or animals

sonar—a way of using sound to navigate, measure or communicate with other objects or locate them underwater

species—a group of living things that are similar to each other and breed with each other, not other species

tentacles—long limbs that some species use to move around in the water, grab things or even stun other creatures

venom—a poisonous substance produced by an animal and delivered through a bite or sting

To my special friend Abdul and everyone brave enough to be scared.
Thanks also to Dr. Darryl Gwynne for your invaluable input. —E.S.

For Lonan. This book is dedicated to you, my favorite blackbird. —H.M.

Text copyright © Erin Silver 2024
Illustrations copyright © Hayden Maynard 2024

Published in Canada and the United States in 2024 by Orca Book Publishers.
orcabook.com

All rights reserved. No part of this publication may be reproduced or transmitted in any form or by any means, electronic or mechanical, including photocopying, recording or by any information storage and retrieval system now known or to be invented, without permission in writing from the publisher.

Library and Archives Canada Cataloguing in Publication

Title: Mighty scared : the amazing ways animals defend themselves when they're afraid / Erin Silver; illustrated by Hayden Maynard.
Names: Silver, Erin, 1980– author. | Maynard, Hayden, illustrator.
Identifiers: Canadiana (print) 2023018765X | Canadiana (ebook) 20230187668 |
ISBN 9781459836068 (hardcover) | ISBN 9781459836075 (PDF) | ISBN 9781459836082 (EPUB)
Subjects: LCSH: Animal defenses—Juvenile literature. | LCSH: Fear in animals—Juvenile literature.
Classification: LCC QL759 .S55 2024 | DDC j591.47—dc23

Library of Congress Control Number: 2023934242

Summary: This illustrated nonfiction picture book explores the unique and disgusting things that animals do when they're scared.

Orca Book Publishers is committed to reducing the consumption of nonrenewable resources in the production of our books. We make every effort to use materials that support a sustainable future.

Orca Book Publishers gratefully acknowledges the support for its publishing programs provided by the following agencies: the Government of Canada, the Canada Council for the Arts and the Province of British Columbia through the BC Arts Council and the Book Publishing Tax Credit.

The author and publisher have made every effort to ensure that the information in this book was correct at the time of publication. The author and publisher do not assume any liability for any loss, damage, or disruption caused by errors or omissions. Every effort has been made to trace copyright holders and to obtain their permission for the use of copyrighted material. The publisher apologizes for any errors or omissions and would be grateful if notified of any corrections that should be incorporated in future reprints or editions of this book.

Cover and interior artwork by Hayden Maynard
Edited by Kirstie Hudson
Design by Rachel Page

Printed and bound in South Korea.

27 26 25 24 • 1 2 3 4

ERIN SILVER is the author of several books for young readers, including *Good Food, Bad Waste: Let's Eat for the Planet*, *Sitting Shiva* and *Rush Hour: Navigating Our Global Traffic Jam*. Erin's journalistic work has appeared in everything from the *Washington Post* and the *Globe and Mail* to *Harper's Bazaar* and *Good Housekeeping*. She has a postgraduate journalism degree and an MFA in creative nonfiction from King's College. Erin lives in Toronto.

HAYDEN MAYNARD is a Canadian illustrator who graduated from Sheridan College's Illustration program. His clients include the *New York Times*, *The Walrus*, the *Globe and Mail*, *Reader's Digest* and the *Washington Post*. Hayden lives in Kingston, Ontario.